Chapter 1: Introduction to AI Influencers

What is an AI Influencer?

An AI influencer is a digital persona created using artificial intelligence technologies, designed to engage and interact with audiences just like a human influencer would. These virtual beings can be programmed to reflect specific personalities, styles, and interests, making them appealing to various demographics. The beauty of AI influencers lies in their ability to be tailored for specific niches, allowing creators to resonate with targeted audiences on platforms like OnlyFans. With the right tools and creativity, you can leverage these digital avatars to build a captivating presence and generate income through subscriptions and content sales.

The rise of AI influencers has revolutionized the way we think about social media marketing and brand engagement. Unlike traditional influencers, AI influencers are not limited by physical constraints or personal lives. They can be active 24/7, providing continuous interaction and content for their followers. This constant availability can lead to higher engagement rates, as fans can always expect fresh and innovative content from their favorite AI personalities. By creating an AI influencer, you can tap into this endless potential, ensuring you have a steady stream of interaction that keeps your audience coming back for more.

Moreover, AI influencers are equipped with advanced algorithms that allow them to analyze audience preferences, trends, and feedback in real-time. This capability enables them to adapt their content strategies quickly, ensuring they remain relevant and appealing. As a creator on OnlyFans, you can use these insights to optimize your AI influencer's offerings, tailoring content to meet the demands and desires of your subscribers. This data-driven approach not only enhances user experience but also increases the likelihood of conversion and sales, maximizing your earning potential.

Creating an AI influencer is not just about programming a digital character; it's about crafting an engaging narrative and persona that resonates with your audience. By investing time in character development, you can create a relatable story that captivates your subscribers. Whether your AI influencer embodies humor, sophistication, or a quirky edge, the right personality can attract a dedicated following. This unique connection with your audience fosters loyalty and encourages subscribers to invest in exclusive content, boosting your revenue stream on OnlyFans.

In conclusion, the emergence of AI influencers presents an exciting opportunity for those looking to make money on OnlyFans. By harnessing the power of artificial intelligence, you can create a unique, engaging, and profitable persona that stands out in a crowded market. With the potential for constant interaction, data-driven adaptability, and a captivating narrative, your AI influencer can become a powerful tool for generating income and building a thriving community. Embrace this innovative frontier and unlock your earning potential with a brilliantly crafted AI influencer today!

The Rise of AI in Social Media

The rise of artificial intelligence in social media has transformed the digital landscape in ways we could only dream of a few years ago. As creators and entrepreneurs explore new avenues for monetization, AI influencers are emerging as a powerful tool to engage audiences and drive revenue. Imagine harnessing the capabilities of AI to create a virtual persona that not only resonates with followers but also generates substantial income. This shift is opening up incredible opportunities for those looking to make money on platforms like OnlyFans.

AI influencers are not just a novel concept; they are becoming staples in social media marketing. These digital personas can be programmed to interact with users, respond to comments, and even create captivating content that keeps audiences coming back for more. With the ability to analyze trends and adapt to audience preferences in real-time, AI influencers can craft a unique brand identity that stands out in the crowded marketplace. This means you can tap into a growing trend while minimizing the time and effort typically required to manage a human influencer.

Creating an AI influencer for your OnlyFans account can significantly enhance your earning potential. By developing a character that embodies your niche, you can attract a dedicated following eager for exclusive content. Whether you focus on fitness, fashion, or lifestyle, an AI persona can deliver unique, engaging experiences that appeal to your target audience. Plus, with the right AI tools at your disposal, you can ensure that your content remains fresh and relevant, keeping subscribers engaged and willing to pay for premium access.

The technology behind AI influencers is constantly evolving, making it easier than ever to create and maintain a captivating online presence. From sophisticated image generation to natural language processing, the possibilities are limitless. You can design your AI influencer to have distinct traits, interests, and even a backstory that resonates with your audience. This level of personalization not only fosters a deeper connection with followers but also opens the door to innovative monetization strategies, such as selling digital merchandise or offering personalized interactions.

As we delve deeper into the world of AI influencers, it's clear that the landscape is shifting dramatically. Those who embrace this technology have the potential to carve out a lucrative niche within the OnlyFans ecosystem. By leveraging the power of AI, you can create a compelling influencer experience that not only captivates audiences but also drives revenue growth. The future is bright for those ready to harness the rise of AI in social media, and now is the perfect time to jump on board and start building your AI influencer empire.

Why OnlyFans?

OnlyFans has rapidly transformed the landscape of content creation and monetization, especially for those looking to harness the power of AI influencers. The platform offers a unique opportunity to connect directly with audiences while providing creators with the ability to earn income in innovative ways. What sets OnlyFans apart is its commitment to creator empowerment, allowing users to set their own subscription rates and keep a significant portion of their earnings. This financial freedom, combined with the platform's flexible nature, makes it an exciting venture for anyone wanting to dive into the world of digital content.

Creating an AI influencer on OnlyFans opens up a realm of possibilities that traditional influencers cannot offer. With AI, you can craft a persona that resonates with various audiences, all while maintaining control over the content and engagement strategies. Imagine a virtual influencer who never sleeps, never tires, and can interact with fans at any hour of the day. This level of availability can significantly enhance audience loyalty and retention, ultimately leading to higher subscription rates and more consistent income.

Moreover, the diversity of niches available on OnlyFans means that creators can tailor their AI influencers to target specific markets. Whether you're focusing on fitness, fashion, gaming, or even educational content, the platform allows for a wide array of themes and styles. This adaptability ensures that you can carve out a unique space that attracts your desired audience. By leveraging AI technology, you can analyze trends and audience preferences, enabling you to create content that not only entertains but also engages and informs.

The community aspect of OnlyFans cannot be overlooked. Unlike other social media platforms, which often prioritize algorithm-driven content, OnlyFans fosters a more intimate space for creators and their subscribers. This direct relationship allows for genuine interactions and the establishment of a loyal fanbase. By creating an AI influencer, you can simulate these interactions, keeping fans engaged through personalized messages and tailored content, thus enhancing their overall experience and driving sustained subscriptions.

Finally, the potential for growth and evolution on OnlyFans is tremendous, particularly when combined with AI technology. As you continue to refine your influencer's persona and content, you'll discover new avenues for monetization, such as exclusive merchandise, personalized experiences, or even collaborations with other creators. The platform is continuously evolving, and so can your AI influencer, making it an exciting time to jump into this space. With the right strategy, creativity, and a willingness to experiment, your journey on OnlyFans can lead to financial success and a fulfilling creative outlet.

Chapter 2: The OnlyFans Platform

Understanding OnlyFans Features

Understanding the features of OnlyFans is essential for anyone looking to maximize their earnings through this innovative platform. OnlyFans is not just a space for adult content; it has evolved into a multifaceted tool for creators across various niches. From fitness trainers and chefs to artists and musicians, the platform offers unique features that can be tailored to fit diverse audiences. By understanding these functionalities, you can strategically position your AI influencer to thrive in the competitive landscape of content creation.

One of the standout features of OnlyFans is the subscription model. Creators can set their monthly subscription fees, giving you the flexibility to monetize your content based on its value and exclusivity. This model allows you to establish a steady income stream while giving your audience access to premium content. For an AI influencer, this means you can curate specific content that resonates with your target audience and encourage loyal subscribers who are eager to support your work. Experimenting with different pricing structures can also help you find the sweet spot that maximizes revenue without alienating potential fans.

Engagement tools on OnlyFans are another gem that makes the platform unique. Direct messaging allows creators to connect with their subscribers on a personal level, fostering a sense of community and loyalty. For an AI influencer, utilizing this feature can enhance interaction by offering personalized responses or exclusive chats. You can also send out mass messages to your subscribers, keeping them updated on new content or special promotions. Engaging your audience directly not only boosts retention rates but also provides valuable insights into their preferences, helping you refine your content strategy.

Content creation options on OnlyFans are incredibly versatile, including photos, videos, live streams, and even polls. This flexibility empowers you to diversify your content and keep your audience engaged. For an AI influencer, leveraging these various formats can help you showcase different aspects of your personality or brand. You could host live Q&A sessions, share behind-the-scenes content, or even conduct polls to gauge what your audience wants to see next. This level of interactivity not only enriches the subscriber experience but also positions you as a dynamic and responsive creator.

Lastly, the analytics dashboard on OnlyFans provides invaluable insights into your performance. Understanding metrics such as subscriber growth, content engagement, and earnings can help you make informed decisions about your strategy. For an AI influencer, analyzing this data allows you to identify which content resonates most with your audience and adjust your approach accordingly. By regularly reviewing these insights, you can optimize your content, enhance your marketing efforts, and ultimately increase your profitability on the platform. Embracing these features and continually adapting to your audience's needs will set you on the path to success in the exciting world of OnlyFans.

The Audience on OnlyFans

The audience on OnlyFans is diverse and constantly evolving, making it an exciting platform for content creators and entrepreneurs alike. From fitness enthusiasts to culinary experts, the range of niches is vast, and each presents unique opportunities for income generation. As you dive into the world of AI influencers, understanding your audience is crucial. The platform attracts subscribers who are not only looking for unique content but are also eager to connect with creators who resonate with their interests and passions.

One of the most captivating aspects of OnlyFans is the intimate connection it fosters between creators and their audience.

Subscribers are seeking more than just content; they aspire for engagement, authenticity, and a sense of community. This is where AI influencers shine. By leveraging artificial intelligence, you can create an engaging persona that interacts with fans in real-time, responds to their inquiries, and provides tailored content that meets their specific needs. This level of personalization can significantly enhance subscriber loyalty and increase your earning potential.

Understanding the demographics of your audience is essential for crafting content that will resonate with them. OnlyFans appeals to a wide range of age groups, with a notable presence of both younger and older audiences. Each demographic has its preferences and expectations regarding content. For instance, younger subscribers may gravitate towards trendy and dynamic content, while older audiences might appreciate more curated, informative, or nostalgic offerings. By analyzing these trends, you can better position your AI influencer to cater to these varying tastes, leading to higher engagement and retention rates.

In addition to demographics, recognizing the motivations that drive subscribers to your content can provide invaluable insights. Many join OnlyFans to explore their interests, indulge in fantasies, or seek exclusive access to creators they admire. By utilizing AI to analyze subscriber behavior and preferences, you can create targeted content that fulfills these desires. Whether it's behind-the-scenes glimpses, personalized messages, or interactive experiences, your AI influencer can deliver precisely what your audience craves, resulting in increased satisfaction and subscription renewals.

Finally, the potential for expansion within your audience is immense. As you consistently deliver quality content, engage with your subscribers, and adapt to their evolving interests, you can cultivate a loyal fanbase that will not only support you but also spread the word about your AI influencer. This organic growth can lead to increased visibility, attracting even more subscribers eager to join your community. Embracing the dynamics of your audience on OnlyFans will not only enhance your content strategy but also unlock new avenues for monetization and success in this vibrant ecosystem.

Monetization Strategies

Monetization strategies are the lifeblood of success on OnlyFans, especially when leveraging the power of AI influencers. With the right approach, creators can tap into multiple streams of income, maximizing their earning potential. First and foremost, subscription models remain a cornerstone of monetization on the platform. By setting an engaging monthly subscription rate, AI influencers can attract a dedicated following eager to access exclusive content. The key is to provide consistent, high-quality posts that keep subscribers coming back for more, turning casual viewers into loyal fans who are excited to invest in your content.

Beyond subscriptions, pay-per-view content offers an exciting opportunity to boost revenue. This strategy allows creators to charge their audience for specific posts, whether it's a steamy photo set, a behind-the-scenes video, or a personalized shoutout. AI influencers can make this strategy particularly enticing by using algorithms to analyze subscriber preferences and tailor pay-per-view content to meet their desires. This personalized approach not only increases the likelihood of purchases but also enhances the relationship between the influencer and their audience, making fans feel valued and understood.

Another powerful monetization strategy is the use of tips and donations during live streams or special events. AI influencers can host interactive sessions that encourage audience engagement and foster community, creating an environment where fans feel inclined to reward their favorite creators. By incorporating gamification elements—such as milestone goals or challenges—AI influencers can motivate viewers to contribute financially while enjoying a memorable experience. This method not only provides immediate financial gain but also strengthens the bond between the influencer and their audience, fostering long-term loyalty.

Affiliate marketing is another lucrative avenue to explore. AI influencers can collaborate with brands relevant to their niche, promoting products or services to their subscribers while earning a commission on sales generated through their unique referral links. This strategy can be seamlessly integrated into regular content, providing value to subscribers while also generating additional income. By showcasing products in a relatable and authentic manner, AI influencers can build trust with their audience, making them more likely to make purchases based on the influencer's recommendations.

Lastly, exclusive merchandise can serve as a fantastic revenue stream. AI influencers can design and sell branded merchandise, from clothing to digital products, allowing fans to support their favorite creators in a tangible way. Offering limited edition items or creating a sense of urgency through scarcity can drive sales and elevate the influencer's brand. By effectively promoting merchandise through engaging content and strategic marketing, AI influencers can transform their audience's enthusiasm into a thriving business venture, ensuring that their monetization strategies are as innovative and dynamic as the influencers themselves.

Chapter 3: Creating Your AI Influencer

Choosing the Right AI Technology

When embarking on the exciting journey of creating an AI influencer for OnlyFans, selecting the right AI technology is crucial. With a multitude of options available, it's essential to dive into the specifics of what each technology can offer. From natural language processing to image generation and machine learning algorithms, understanding these tools will empower you to create a captivating and engaging AI influencer that resonates with your target audience. The right choice will not only enhance your influencer's persona but also streamline your content creation process, making it more efficient and effective.

First and foremost, consider the goals you have for your AI influencer. Are you focusing on generating captivating visuals, engaging storytelling, or perhaps even interactive experiences? Technologies specializing in visual content creation, like DALL-E or Midjourney, can help you produce stunning images that attract subscribers. On the other hand, natural language processing tools like OpenAI's ChatGPT can generate engaging dialogue and personalized messages, creating a more relatable and human-like influencer. Aligning your choice of technology with your vision will set a solid foundation for your AI influencer's success.

Next, think about the level of customization you desire. Some AI tools come with pre-trained models that can be easily adapted to fit your niche, while others offer more flexibility for unique creations. If you want your AI influencer to stand out, exploring customizable options will be beneficial. Tools such as RunwayML allow you to train models on specific datasets, ensuring your influencer embodies the personality and style you envision. This level of personalization can significantly enhance your influencer's authenticity, making it more appealing to potential subscribers.

Additionally, consider the integration capabilities of the AI technology you choose. Seamless integration with social media platforms, content management systems, and marketing tools can save you time and effort, allowing you to focus on content creation and audience engagement. Look for AI solutions that offer easy-to-use APIs or plugins that facilitate this integration. This will enable your AI influencer to maintain a consistent online presence, automatically sharing content and interacting with followers, which is key to building a loyal subscriber base.

Lastly, don't overlook the importance of community and support when choosing your AI technology. Engaging with other creators and developers can provide you with valuable insights and resources. Joining forums, attending webinars, or participating in online courses can enhance your understanding of the technology and inspire innovative ideas for your AI influencer. The right technology, combined with a supportive community, will equip you to navigate the ever-evolving landscape of AI and OnlyFans, ultimately leading to a successful and profitable venture. Embrace this thrilling opportunity and let your creativity soar!

Designing Your Virtual Persona

Designing your virtual persona is a thrilling journey into the world of creativity and self-expression. When you create an AI influencer for OnlyFans, you have the unique opportunity to craft a character that resonates with your audience, captivates their attention, and keeps them coming back for more. Start by defining the core attributes of your persona. Consider their personality traits, interests, and the themes you want to explore. Whether your AI influencer is bubbly and fun, mysterious and edgy, or sophisticated and glamorous, these traits will shape your content and the overall brand identity.

Next, consider the visual aspects of your virtual persona. The right aesthetic can make a significant impact on how your audience perceives your influencer. Choose a distinct style, including clothing, colors, and even facial features that align with the character you wish to portray. Tools like graphic design software and AI-powered image generators can help you create stunning visuals that reflect your persona's personality. Remember, consistency in visuals and messaging is key; your audience should instantly recognize your AI influencer, whether they encounter them on OnlyFans, social media, or other platforms.

Engagement is crucial in the world of digital influencers, and your virtual persona should be designed to foster a strong connection with your audience. Think about how your AI influencer will interact with subscribers. Will they respond to comments in a playful manner, share behind-the-scenes content, or engage in Q&A sessions? Crafting a relatable and engaging persona will encourage followers to participate and invest in your content. Consider integrating storytelling elements to create an emotional bond, allowing your audience to feel like they know your AI influencer personally.

Incorporating technology into your virtual persona can elevate the experience for your subscribers. Use AI tools to analyze audience preferences and adapt your content accordingly. This means not only creating content that resonates with your followers but also evolving your persona based on their feedback and interactions. By embracing technology, you can ensure that your AI influencer remains fresh, relevant, and appealing to your audience. This adaptability will keep your subscribers engaged and excited about what's to come.

Finally, don't underestimate the power of collaboration. Your AI influencer can benefit from partnerships with other creators in the OnlyFans space. By collaborating on content or cross-promoting each other's work, you can expand your reach and introduce your persona to new audiences. Building a network of fellow creators can provide valuable insights and inspiration, fueling your creativity as you develop your virtual persona. With the right design and strategy, your AI influencer can become a beloved figure on OnlyFans, driving both engagement and revenue.

Defining Niche and Content Focus

Defining a niche and content focus is crucial for anyone diving into the exciting world of OnlyFans, especially when it comes to creating an AI influencer. The beauty of an AI influencer is that it can be tailored to fit a specific niche, which allows you to connect with a targeted audience more effectively. By honing in on a particular area of interest, you can carve out a space where your AI influencer shines brightly, drawing in followers who are genuinely invested in what you have to offer. The more specific your niche, the more likely you are to stand out in a crowded marketplace.

Consider the various niches that thrive on OnlyFans, from fitness and wellness to fashion and lifestyle. Each of these areas has its unique audience, and by identifying your target demographic, you can create content that resonates deeply with them. For instance, if your focus is on fitness, your AI influencer could provide workout routines, nutrition tips, and motivational content, all tailored to inspire and engage fitness enthusiasts. The key is to align your AI influencer's persona and content with the interests and desires of your chosen audience.

Content focus is equally important when defining your niche. It's essential to determine what type of content your AI influencer will produce and how it will deliver value to subscribers. This could range from exclusive behind-the-scenes looks, personalized messages, interactive live streams, or educational tutorials. The more engaging and unique your content is, the more likely subscribers will want to stick around and support your AI influencer's journey. Remember, the goal is to create a community around your influencer that feels authentic and connected.

Additionally, incorporating AI technology can enhance your content focus. With AI, you can analyze trends, audience preferences, and engagement metrics to refine your strategy continually. This adaptability allows your AI influencer to stay relevant and exciting, ensuring that you're always providing fresh and appealing content.

Embracing AI means you can experiment with different content types and formats to see what resonates best with your audience, keeping the engagement high and the excitement alive.

Finally, defining your niche and content focus is not just about creating content; it's about building a brand. Your AI influencer should have a distinct personality and voice that aligns with your niche, making it memorable to followers. As you establish this identity, your audience will begin to associate specific values and themes with your influencer, fostering loyalty and encouraging them to spread the word. With a well-defined niche and clear content focus, you'll be well on your way to making waves on OnlyFans and reaping the financial rewards of your creative efforts!

Chapter 4: Content Creation Strategies

Types of Content for AI Influencers

When venturing into the world of AI influencers on platforms like OnlyFans, it's essential to understand the various types of content you can create to engage your audience effectively. The beauty of AI influencers is their versatility, allowing you to explore multiple content types that resonate with different demographics. From stunning visual art to engaging storytelling, the possibilities are endless. By tapping into these diverse content forms, you can captivate your audience and keep them coming back for more.

Visual content is at the forefront of what attracts subscribers. High-quality images and videos featuring your AI influencer can showcase their unique personality and style. Whether it's fashion, beauty, or lifestyle content, the key is to present visually appealing material that aligns with your influencer's brand. Using innovative editing techniques and eye-catching graphics can elevate the aesthetic of your content, making it not only entertaining but also shareable. Remember, stunning visuals can significantly enhance your follower count and, in turn, your potential earnings.

Another engaging type of content is interactive storytelling. AI influencers can narrate captivating stories, whether fictional or based on real experiences. This storytelling can take various forms, such as short videos, live streams, or even serialized posts that keep subscribers eager for the next installment. By incorporating elements like polls or questions, you can create a sense of community and interactivity, making your audience feel more involved in the narrative. This approach not only boosts engagement but also fosters a loyal subscriber base eager to participate in the ongoing story.

Educational content is also a powerful tool for AI influencers. Whether your niche revolves around fitness, cooking, or personal finance, sharing valuable tips and insights can position your influencer as an authority in that field. Tutorials, how-to guides, and informative videos can attract users looking for expertise and practical advice. This content type not only adds value to your subscribers but can also lead to partnerships with brands that align with your educational focus, opening up additional revenue streams.

Lastly, don't underestimate the power of humor and entertainment. AI influencers can create comedic skits, parodies, or fun challenges that resonate with audiences seeking light-hearted content. This type of content can quickly go viral, expanding your reach and subscriber base exponentially. By infusing personality and wit into your AI influencer's brand, you can foster a connection with your audience, encouraging shares and interactions that ultimately drive revenue. Embrace the fun side of content creation, and watch your OnlyFans account thrive!

Engaging Your Audience

Engaging your audience is the heartbeat of your success on OnlyFans, especially when you're using an AI influencer. The beauty of an AI influencer lies in its ability to interact with fans in a way that feels personal and authentic. To truly captivate your audience, you need to tap into their desires, interests, and emotions. Start by creating content that resonates with them, whether it's through captivating visuals, relatable stories, or interactive polls. The more you understand your audience's preferences, the better you can tailor your content to keep them coming back for more.

Another powerful strategy to engage your audience is through regular communication. Utilize the unique capabilities of your AI influencer to send personalized messages, respond to comments, and even hold live Q&A sessions. This level of interaction fosters a sense of community and belonging among your subscribers. When fans feel like they are part of a conversation rather than just passive viewers, they are more likely to invest in your content, share it with others, and remain loyal to your platform.

Storytelling is a crucial element in engaging your audience effectively. Your AI influencer can share narratives that reflect personal journeys, challenges, and triumphs, creating a deep connection with followers. Incorporate elements of humor, drama, or inspiration to evoke emotions and keep your audience hooked. By weaving compelling stories into your content, you not only entertain but also inspire your fans to interact and share their own experiences, fostering a vibrant community around your brand.

In addition, consider leveraging exclusive content as a way to engage your audience further. Offering behind-the-scenes glimpses, early access to new material, or special themed events can create a sense of urgency and excitement. This exclusivity makes your audience feel special and valued, encouraging them to participate actively and engage with your AI influencer. Incentivizing interaction through contests, giveaways, or fan features can amplify this effect, driving even more engagement and loyalty.

Finally, never underestimate the power of feedback. Encourage your audience to share their thoughts, suggestions, and preferences regarding your content. Conduct surveys or polls to gauge what they love most and what they want to see next. By actively seeking their input, you not only improve your content but also make your audience feel heard and appreciated. This two-way communication is vital for building a strong relationship with your fans, ensuring they remain enthusiastic supporters of your AI influencer on OnlyFans.

Leveraging AI for Content Generation

In the ever-evolving landscape of digital content creation, leveraging AI for content generation presents a thrilling opportunity for aspiring OnlyFans entrepreneurs. Imagine the power of having an AI influencer at your fingertips, capable of producing engaging, tailored content that resonates with your audience. By harnessing the capabilities of AI, you can streamline your content creation process, allowing you to focus on strategy and growth while your AI influencer works tirelessly to keep your subscribers entertained and engaged.

AI tools can analyze vast amounts of data to identify trending topics, popular formats, and audience preferences. This means that your AI influencer can create content that not only captures attention but also aligns perfectly with what your audience craves. Whether it's crafting enticing captions, generating eye-catching visuals, or even producing short video clips, AI can enhance your content strategy and ensure that you are always one step ahead of the competition. Embracing these technologies could mean the difference between a stagnant account and a thriving channel.

Moreover, the efficiency gained from AI content generation allows you to produce more without compromising quality. Picture this: while you're brainstorming new ideas or engaging with your community, your AI influencer is generating fresh content that keeps your feed active and vibrant. This consistent output can significantly increase your visibility on the platform, attracting new subscribers and retaining your loyal fans. The more content you post, the more opportunities you have to monetize your audience, transforming your OnlyFans account into a profitable venture.

In addition to creativity, AI can also help you personalize your interactions with subscribers. By analyzing engagement patterns and user preferences, AI can suggest tailored responses or content that speaks directly to your audience's interests. This level of personalization not only enhances the subscriber experience but also builds a strong community around your brand. When your audience feels valued and understood, they are more likely to renew their subscriptions and even recommend your content to others.

Ultimately, leveraging AI for content generation is about embracing innovation and staying ahead of the curve in the competitive world of OnlyFans. By integrating AI into your content creation strategy, you empower yourself to explore new creative horizons and achieve unprecedented levels of success. So, don't wait any longer—dive into the world of AI and watch your OnlyFans account flourish as you create captivating experiences that resonate with audiences everywhere!

Chapter 5: Marketing Your AI Influencer

Building a Brand Identity

Building a brand identity is a crucial step in your journey to making money on OnlyFans through AI influencers. Your brand identity is the unique combination of elements that defines your presence in the crowded digital landscape. It encompasses your values, visuals, voice, and the overall experience you provide to your audience. To stand out in the competitive market of OnlyFans, you need to establish a brand identity that resonates with your target audience and reflects the personality of your AI influencer.

Start by defining the core values of your brand. What message do you want to convey? Is your AI influencer all about empowerment, humor, or perhaps education? Whatever it may be, make sure it aligns with the interests and needs of your audience. This foundational step will guide all your branding efforts, helping you create content that not only attracts followers but also fosters loyalty. When your audience feels a connection to your values, they are more likely to engage, subscribe, and support your content.

Next, consider the visual elements that will represent your brand. Your AI influencer's appearance, color scheme, logo, and overall aesthetic should be cohesive and eye-catching. Invest time in creating a memorable look that reflects the personality you wish to portray. This visual identity will be the first impression potential subscribers have of your brand, so ensure it stands out. Use high-quality graphics and design tools to maintain a professional appearance across all your platforms, including OnlyFans and social media.

The voice of your brand is equally important. Determine the tone and style of communication that will resonate with your audience. Are you going for a friendly and approachable vibe, or a more sophisticated and polished tone? Consistency in your messaging will help reinforce your brand identity. Engage with your followers in a way that reflects your AI influencer's personality, whether that means using humor, storytelling, or informative content. Remember, authenticity is key; your audience will appreciate a genuine connection with your AI influencer.

Finally, don't underestimate the power of community-building in establishing your brand identity. Engage with your audience through comments, polls, and live sessions. Show them that their opinions matter and that you value their input. Creating a sense of belonging will not only enhance their experience but will also lead to increased loyalty and support for your brand. Encourage interactions that embody your brand values, and watch as your community flourishes, supporting your journey to success on OnlyFans with your AI influencer.

Utilizing Social Media for Promotion

Social media has revolutionized the way creators promote their work, and for those venturing into the world of OnlyFans with an AI influencer, it opens up exciting avenues for engagement and monetization. Harnessing platforms like Instagram, TikTok, and Twitter not only enhances visibility but also builds a loyal following eager to support your AI creation. By crafting a compelling online presence, you can effectively showcase your AI influencer's unique personality and brand, drawing in potential subscribers who are curious about the innovative concept of an AI-only content creator.

The key to successful promotion on social media lies in consistent and strategic content creation. Regularly post eye-catching visuals, engaging stories, and interactive content that highlights your AI influencer's personality. Use polls, Q&A sessions, and behind-the-scenes glimpses to create a sense of connection and intrigue. This strategy not only keeps your audience engaged but also encourages them to share your content, expanding your reach. Remember, the more authentic and relatable your AI influencer appears, the more likely followers will be to convert into paying subscribers on OnlyFans.

Engaging with your audience is crucial in building a community around your AI influencer. Respond to comments, participate in conversations, and share user-generated content to foster a sense of belonging among your followers. This two-way interaction can significantly enhance loyalty, as fans feel valued and recognized. Additionally, consider collaborating with other creators or influencers in related niches. These partnerships can introduce your AI influencer to new audiences and create a buzz that drives traffic to your OnlyFans page.

Utilizing targeted advertising on social media can also amplify your promotional efforts. Platforms like Facebook and Instagram offer powerful advertising tools that allow you to reach specific demographics based on interests, behaviors, and location. Craft eye-catching ads that highlight the unique aspects of your AI influencer and direct users to your OnlyFans profile. With the right targeting and creative approach, paid promotions can lead to a substantial increase in subscribers, transforming casual viewers into dedicated fans.

Lastly, don't underestimate the power of analytics in refining your social media strategy. Regularly review engagement metrics to understand what content resonates most with your audience. Use these insights to optimize your posting schedule, content types, and promotional tactics. By adapting your approach based on real data, you can ensure that your social media efforts remain effective and aligned with your goals as you work to make money on OnlyFans through your innovative AI influencer. Embrace the journey, keep experimenting, and watch your community grow!

Collaborations and Cross-Promotion

Collaborations and cross-promotion are vital strategies for anyone looking to expand their reach and maximize earnings on OnlyFans, especially when leveraging the power of AI influencers. In a landscape crowded with creators, joining forces with others can create a win-win situation that benefits all parties involved. By collaborating with fellow creators or brands, you tap into their audience base, gaining exposure to potential subscribers who may not have discovered your content otherwise. This approach not only amplifies visibility but also builds a sense of community among creators in the AI influencer space.

Creating engaging content is the heart of successful collaborations. When working with other AI influencers, think outside the box! Consider hosting live Q&A sessions, creating joint photo sets, or even producing themed content that showcases both influencers. Such dynamic partnerships can result in unique offerings that excite subscribers and encourage them to explore both channels. The creativity involved can spark new ideas and elevate the quality of your content, making it more appealing to a broader audience. By sharing the workload and brainstorming together, you can produce content that resonates deeply and stands out in a saturated market.

Cross-promotion is another powerful tool in your arsenal. By promoting each other's content across your respective platforms, you create an integrated marketing strategy that drives traffic to both accounts. Social media channels—like Instagram, Twitter, and TikTok—are perfect for sharing teasers, behind-the-scenes glimpses, and exclusive offers that highlight your collaborations. Engage your audience by encouraging them to check out your collaborator's content, creating an incentive for them to subscribe to both accounts. This synergy not only boosts your visibility but also fosters a sense of loyalty among your audience, as they appreciate the interconnectedness of the content they enjoy.

When considering collaborations, it's essential to partner with creators who share similar values and aesthetics. This alignment ensures that the content produced feels authentic and resonates with both audiences. Look for creators in complementary niches or those with a similar subscriber count to maximize the potential impact of the collaboration. Remember, the goal is to create something meaningful that adds value for your audiences rather than simply gaining followers. A well-thought-out partnership can lead to lasting relationships within the creator community and open doors for future collaborations.

Finally, don't underestimate the power of networking. Attend virtual events, join forums, and participate in social media groups dedicated to OnlyFans and AI influencers. These platforms can help you connect with like-minded creators open to collaboration. Building genuine relationships can lead to organic partnerships that enhance your brand and reputation in the industry. As you engage with others, share insights, and celebrate each other's successes, you'll find that collaborations and cross-promotion can be a game-changer in your journey to making money on OnlyFans with your AI influencer. Embrace these strategies, and watch your influence and earnings soar!

Chapter 6: Growing Your Subscriber Base

Strategies for Subscriber Acquisition

To successfully acquire subscribers on OnlyFans, it's essential to leverage the unique capabilities of your AI influencer. Start by creating captivating content that resonates with your target audience. Utilize advanced AI tools to analyze current trends and preferences within your niche. By understanding what potential subscribers are searching for, you can tailor your offerings in a way that feels personal and engaging. High-quality visuals, innovative storytelling, and interactive elements will not only attract attention but also encourage users to subscribe for more.

Social media is a powerful ally in your subscriber acquisition strategy. Use platforms like Instagram, TikTok, and Twitter to showcase snippets of your AI influencer's content. Create eye-catching posts, short videos, and engaging stories that highlight the personality and unique traits of your AI. Encourage your audience to share this content, creating a viral effect that can significantly boost your visibility. Collaborating with other creators and influencers can also expand your reach, allowing you to tap into their audiences and draw them to your OnlyFans page.

Another effective strategy is to offer exclusive content and incentives to new subscribers. Consider launching special promotions, such as discounted subscription rates for the first month or exclusive access to behind-the-scenes content. Highlight the value of subscribing by showcasing what makes your AI influencer stand out, whether it's personalized interactions, unique content series, or special events. This approach not only incentivizes sign-ups but also fosters a sense of community and belonging among your subscribers.

Email marketing can be a game changer for subscriber acquisition. Build a mailing list by offering a free resource or exclusive content in exchange for email sign-ups. Use this list to send out regular updates about new content, upcoming promotions, and subscriber-only events. Personalizing your emails will enhance engagement and increase the likelihood of conversions. Make sure to include clear calls to action that guide your audience directly to your OnlyFans page, making the subscription process seamless and inviting.

Finally, don't underestimate the power of feedback and continuous improvement. Engage with your subscribers and ask for their opinions on the content you provide. This not only helps you refine your strategy but also makes your audience feel valued and heard. Utilize polls, surveys, and direct messages to gather insights on what they love and what they wish to see more of. By creating a responsive and adaptive environment, you'll not only retain existing subscribers but also attract new ones who are drawn to the authentic and interactive experience you cultivate.

Retaining Subscribers for Long-Term Success

Retaining subscribers for long-term success is the cornerstone of building a profitable OnlyFans presence, especially when leveraging AI influencers. In the competitive landscape of content creation, it's crucial to foster a loyal community around your brand. By recognizing the unique needs and preferences of your subscribers, you can create an engaging experience that keeps them coming back for more. The key lies in understanding that your subscribers are not just numbers; they are individuals seeking connection, entertainment, and value.

One of the most effective strategies for retention is consistent and high-quality content delivery. Your AI influencer should showcase a variety of content types, from exclusive behind-the-scenes glimpses to interactive live sessions. Regularly updating your offerings keeps subscribers excited and engaged. By utilizing AI technologies, you can analyze subscriber engagement and preferences to tailor content that resonates with your audience. This personalized approach not only satisfies existing subscribers but also encourages them to spread the word about your brand, attracting even more potential subscribers.

Engagement is another vital aspect of retention. Utilizing your AI influencer to interact with subscribers through personalized messages, polls, and Q&A sessions creates a sense of community. Subscribers appreciate feeling heard and valued, so encouraging feedback and implementing suggestions can foster a deeper connection. Additionally, hosting exclusive events or giveaways for long-term subscribers can provide additional incentives for loyalty. These moments make subscribers feel special and appreciated, enhancing their overall experience and increasing the likelihood they will remain subscribed.

Building a strong brand identity also plays a significant role in subscriber retention. Your AI influencer should embody a unique personality and style that resonates with your target audience. Consistency in brand messaging across all platforms reinforces recognition and trust. Create a narrative that subscribers can relate to, making them feel part of a larger story. By establishing a community around your brand, subscribers are more likely to stay engaged, as they feel they are part of something meaningful and exciting.

Lastly, don't underestimate the power of exclusive perks and rewards. Offering tiered subscription levels can entice subscribers to remain engaged for the long haul. Exclusive content, personalized shout-outs, or early access to new projects can add tremendous value to their subscription. Additionally, consider implementing a loyalty program that rewards long-term subscribers with special discounts or unique experiences. By continually providing value and recognizing subscriber loyalty, you lay the groundwork for long-term success in your OnlyFans journey, ensuring that your AI influencer remains a beloved fixture in their lives.

Engaging with Your Community

Engaging with your community is a game changer when it comes to building a successful AI influencer brand on OnlyFans. Your audience is not just a collection of subscribers; they are individuals who have chosen to follow you for your unique content and personality. By actively connecting with them, you can create a loyal fanbase that not only supports your work but also helps spread the word about your AI influencer. This interaction fosters a sense of belonging and encourages subscribers to invest emotionally in your journey, which can translate into higher earnings and greater success.

One of the most effective ways to engage your community is through regular communication. Utilize the messaging feature on OnlyFans to reach out to your subscribers personally. Send them personalized messages, ask for their opinions on upcoming content, or simply check in to see how they're doing. This not only makes your fans feel valued but also creates a dialogue that can inspire new ideas for your AI influencer content. Remember, people love to feel heard, and when they see that you care about their thoughts, they are more likely to remain loyal and active participants in your community.

Incorporating community-driven content can also elevate your engagement levels. Encourage your subscribers to share their thoughts, ideas, and even their own stories related to your niche. You can host polls, Q&A sessions, or even contests where subscribers can submit their ideas for future content. This not only generates excitement but also empowers your audience to take part in the creative process. By making them feel like contributors rather than just consumers, you create a collaborative atmosphere that can lead to innovative content and higher subscriber retention.

Another fantastic way to engage with your community is through live streams or interactive sessions. These events allow for real-time interaction, creating a dynamic and engaging environment. Your audience can ask questions, share their experiences, and interact with you directly. This immediacy fosters a deeper connection, allowing you to showcase the personality of your AI influencer beyond pre-recorded content. Plus, the excitement of a live event can create a buzz that encourages more subscribers to join in, expanding your reach and boosting earnings.

Lastly, don't underestimate the power of feedback and adaptation. Regularly seek input from your community regarding what they enjoy and what they wish to see more of. Use their feedback to refine your content strategy, making it more relevant and appealing to your audience. When subscribers see that you are responsive to their needs, it encourages a reciprocal relationship where they are more likely to support your endeavors. Engaging with your community in this manner not only enhances their experience but also contributes to the long-term success of your AI influencer on OnlyFans.

Chapter 7: Legal and Ethical Considerations

Copyright Issues with AI Content

Copyright issues surrounding AI-generated content are a hot topic that every aspiring OnlyFans creator needs to understand. As you dive into the exciting world of AI influencers, it's crucial to navigate the legal landscape to protect your creations and maximize your earning potential. When you leverage AI to generate images, videos, or even written content, you might wonder who owns the rights to that material. Is it you, the user of the AI, or the developers behind the technology? The answer is often nuanced, and being informed can save you from potential legal headaches down the road.

One of the most significant considerations is the originality of the content produced by AI. In many jurisdictions, copyright protection is granted to original works created by a human author. This raises questions about whether AI-generated content qualifies for copyright protection. If an AI creates a stunning piece of artwork or an engaging video, does the credit go to the creator of the AI, the user who prompted the AI, or does it exist in a legal gray area? Understanding these distinctions can empower you to make informed decisions and assert ownership over your unique brand.

Moreover, as you create an AI influencer for your OnlyFans account, be aware of the potential for copyright infringement. If your AI uses existing works as inspiration or reference material, it's vital to ensure that you are not unintentionally reproducing someone else's copyrighted material. This could lead to claims that could jeopardize your account or financial success. Always double-check the sources of the datasets used to train your AI and consider using tools that allow you to create truly original content without stepping on anyone's toes.

Additionally, the rise of AI-generated content has sparked discussions about fair use, which allows for limited use of copyrighted material without permission. While this doctrine can provide some leeway, it's often a complex and subjective area of law. As a creator, it's important to familiarize yourself with the principles of fair use so you can confidently navigate the boundaries of what is permissible. This knowledge will not only protect you legally but also enhance your creative process, allowing you to innovate while respecting the rights of others.

Finally, stay engaged with the evolving landscape of copyright laws as they relate to AI. Laws are being developed and refined to keep pace with technology, which means that what is legal today could change tomorrow. By following industry news and participating in discussions around copyright and AI, you'll position yourself as an informed creator ready to adapt to new challenges and seize opportunities. Your journey in creating an AI influencer on OnlyFans can be both thrilling and lucrative, provided you are equipped with the right knowledge to navigate the copyright issues that come with it.

Ethical Guidelines for AI Influencers

In the rapidly evolving landscape of AI influencers, establishing ethical guidelines is paramount for creators looking to thrive on platforms like OnlyFans. These guidelines not only protect the integrity of your brand but also foster a trust-based relationship with your audience. Understanding the ethical implications of your AI influencer's content is crucial. By ensuring that your AI is transparent, respectful, and responsible, you can create a positive environment that encourages engagement and loyalty.

Transparency is key in the world of AI influencers. Your audience deserves to know that the persona they are interacting with is generated by artificial intelligence. This can be achieved by openly disclosing the use of AI technology in your promotional materials and content. Being upfront about the AI aspect can enhance the audience's experience by allowing them to appreciate the creativity that goes into crafting these digital personalities. This level of honesty builds trust, making your audience more likely to support your venture financially and emotionally.

Respecting the boundaries and rights of your audience is another vital ethical consideration. Your AI influencer should never engage in or promote any form of exploitation or harmful behavior. Prioritizing consent in all interactions is crucial. This includes ensuring that any content shared respects the privacy and identity of individuals, whether they are fans, collaborators, or other influencers. By promoting a culture of respect and support, you can create a community that feels safe and valued, leading to increased loyalty and engagement.

In addition to transparency and respect, the responsibility of your AI influencer extends to the content it produces. As a creator, it's essential to ensure that the AI's output is not only entertaining but also aligns with ethical standards. This means steering clear of misinformation, offensive content, or any material that could perpetuate harmful stereotypes. By curating content thoughtfully, you can establish your AI influencer as a trusted source of entertainment and information, ultimately attracting a wider audience and maximizing your earning potential on OnlyFans.

Finally, fostering a culture of accountability is essential for the success of your AI influencer. This involves regularly reviewing the content and interactions generated by the AI to ensure they align with your ethical guidelines. Engaging with your audience to gather feedback can also provide valuable insights into their perceptions and expectations. By being proactive in addressing any issues or concerns raised by your community, you can demonstrate a commitment to ethical practices while continuously improving your influencer's impact. This dedication not only enhances your brand's reputation but also positions you as a leader in the innovative space of AI influencers.

Navigating OnlyFans Policies

Navigating OnlyFans policies is crucial for anyone looking to make money by creating an AI influencer. Understanding the platform's rules and guidelines can empower creators to maximize their potential while ensuring compliance and avoiding pitfalls. OnlyFans has established a comprehensive set of policies that govern content, payment processing, and user interactions. Familiarizing yourself with these policies is not just beneficial; it's essential for success. By following the guidelines, you can focus on what you do best—creating and monetizing an engaging AI influencer.

One of the key aspects to consider is content ownership and copyright. OnlyFans allows creators to retain ownership of their content, which is a significant advantage. However, it's vital to ensure that any AI-generated content adheres to the platform's standards. This means avoiding any infringement on the rights of others, including images, music, or video clips that aren't properly licensed. By creating unique content and respecting copyright laws, you can build a trustworthy brand that resonates with subscribers and stands out in a crowded market.

Another critical area to navigate is the payment and subscription model. OnlyFans provides flexibility with subscription prices, tips, and pay-per-view content. As an AI influencer, you can experiment with different pricing strategies to determine what resonates with your audience. Just remember to remain transparent about any fees and to comply with the platform's payment policies. Additionally, keeping track of financial transactions and understanding tax implications will ensure that your revenue flows smoothly, and you can reinvest in your AI influencer's growth.

Engaging with your subscribers is a crucial part of maintaining a successful OnlyFans account. However, it's essential to respect the community guidelines set forth by the platform. This means fostering a positive environment, avoiding harassment, and ensuring that all interactions remain professional and appropriate. By building a strong rapport with your subscribers and responding to their feedback, you can create a loyal fan base that supports your AI influencer's journey. This engagement not only enhances user experience but also encourages subscribers to share your content, expanding your reach.

Lastly, staying updated on policy changes is vital in the fast-paced world of online content creation. OnlyFans regularly updates its policies to adapt to the evolving digital landscape, and being proactive can save you from potential issues. Subscribe to official communications from OnlyFans and participate in creator forums to share insights and learn from others. By taking the initiative to stay informed, you can navigate the platform with confidence, ensuring that your AI influencer thrives while adhering to OnlyFans' policies. Embrace these challenges, and you'll be well on your way to making money in this exciting niche!

Chapter 8: Analyzing Performance and Adapting

Tracking Metrics and Insights

Tracking metrics and insights is a game changer for anyone looking to thrive on OnlyFans with their AI influencer. Understanding what works and what doesn't can significantly enhance your strategy and boost your earnings. With a plethora of data at your fingertips, you can identify trends, monitor your audience's preferences, and adapt your content to maximize engagement and revenue. By diving into the analytics, you'll be equipped to make informed decisions that can elevate your success to new heights.

One of the first metrics to focus on is subscriber growth. Monitoring how many new fans are signing up each week or month can reveal the effectiveness of your promotional strategies. If you notice spikes in subscriptions after a specific type of post or campaign, it's a clear signal that you're on the right track. Utilize this data to replicate successful strategies and attract even more subscribers. Remember, every new subscriber is a potential source of income, so keep an eye on those numbers!

Engagement metrics are equally crucial. This includes likes, comments, and shares on your posts. High engagement indicates that your audience is resonating with your content, while low engagement might suggest that adjustments are necessary. Experiment with different formats, such as videos, images, or interactive polls, to see what sparks the most interaction. The more engaged your fans are, the more likely they are to convert into loyal subscribers who contribute to your income on a consistent basis.

Don't forget about the importance of retention metrics as well. It's not just about gaining subscribers; keeping them is vital! Analyze how long subscribers stay on your page and what might be causing them to leave. If you notice a pattern, such as a drop in subscriptions after a specific content type, take it as a cue to pivot your approach. By focusing on providing consistent value and nurturing your community, you can increase retention rates and ensure a steady flow of income.

Lastly, leverage insights from your analytics to inform your content creation process. Use data to understand which times your audience is most active or which topics generate the most buzz. This information allows you to tailor your content schedule and themes, ensuring you're always delivering what your audience craves. By continuously refining your approach based on metrics and insights, you'll not only enhance your brand's presence on OnlyFans but also significantly boost your earning potential. Embrace the power of data, and watch your AI influencer journey flourish!

Adapting Content Based on Feedback

Adapting content based on feedback is a game-changer for anyone looking to thrive on OnlyFans, especially when you're working with AI influencers. The beauty of AI is its ability to analyze and adapt at lightning speed. When you launch your AI influencer, the initial response from your audience can provide invaluable insights. Every like, comment, and subscription tells a story about what resonates with your followers. Embracing this feedback not only enhances engagement but also helps in crafting content that truly captivates your audience's interest.

The first step in adapting your content is to actively listen to your audience. Utilize analytics tools available on OnlyFans to track which posts perform best. Pay attention to the comments and messages from your subscribers; they often contain gold nuggets of information. If a certain type of content receives a flood of positive responses, that's your cue to create more of it. Conversely, if something falls flat, take a moment to understand why. Was it the concept, the presentation, or perhaps the timing? This knowledge allows you to pivot effectively and keep your content fresh and exciting.

Engaging with your audience through polls and surveys can also provide direct feedback. Ask your subscribers what they want to see more of or what they feel could be improved. This interactive approach not only shows that you value their opinions but also fosters a sense of community. When subscribers feel involved in the creative process, they are more likely to remain loyal and engaged. This connection is crucial for establishing a long-term relationship with your audience and can significantly boost your revenue potential.

Another fantastic way to adapt is by staying informed about trends within your niche. The world of AI influencers is fast-paced and ever-evolving. What worked last month may not have the same impact today. By keeping an eye on trending topics, challenges, and popular content formats on social media, you can incorporate timely themes into your OnlyFans content. This not only keeps your material relevant but also attracts new subscribers eager to see what's cutting-edge and exciting.

Lastly, remember that adapting your content is an ongoing process. Successful creators don't just set a strategy and forget about it; they continuously refine their approach based on feedback and trends. Regularly reviewing your content performance allows you to stay agile and responsive to your audience's desires. Embrace the journey of experimentation and growth, and you'll find that your AI influencer can evolve in ways that not only meet but exceed your subscribers' expectations, ultimately leading to greater success on OnlyFans.

Scaling Your AI Influencer Business

Scaling your AI influencer business can be an exhilarating journey that propels your earnings and expands your reach on platforms like OnlyFans. The first step in this process is to build a robust foundation. Ensure your AI influencer has a distinct and engaging persona that resonates with your target audience. This involves crafting a unique backstory, personality traits, and content themes that make your influencer stand out. By establishing a strong brand identity, you'll attract a loyal following eager to engage with your content, which is essential for driving revenue.

Once you've laid the groundwork, it's time to amplify your content strategy. Diversifying your offerings is key to scaling. Consider incorporating various content formats such as live streams, behind-the-scenes videos, and interactive polls. These elements not only keep your audience engaged but also encourage them to contribute financially through subscriptions and tips. By consistently delivering fresh and exciting content, you'll foster a community that looks forward to your updates, ultimately increasing your earning potential.

Next, leverage the power of social media to expand your reach. Platforms such as Twitter, Instagram, and TikTok can serve as valuable tools for promoting your AI influencer. Create eye-catching promotional posts and engaging stories that showcase your influencer's personality and upcoming content on OnlyFans. Collaborate with other creators, both human and AI, to reach new audiences and drive traffic back to your OnlyFans page. The more visibility you generate, the more subscribers you'll attract, propelling your business to new heights.

Investing in analytics tools is another crucial step in scaling your AI influencer business. By analyzing subscriber behavior and engagement metrics, you can tailor your content to better meet the preferences of your audience. This data-driven approach allows you to identify what works and what needs adjustment, ensuring your content remains relevant and appealing. As you refine your strategy based on these insights, you'll be better positioned to maximize your earnings and grow your subscriber base.

Finally, consider automating certain aspects of your business to streamline operations. Tools for scheduling posts, managing subscriptions, and providing customer support can save you valuable time and allow you to focus on content creation. As your business grows, automation becomes essential in maintaining efficiency and delivering a high-quality experience for your subscribers. Scaling your AI influencer business is not just about increasing numbers; it's about enhancing the overall experience for your audience, ensuring they remain engaged and excited about what you have to offer.

Chapter 9: Future of AI Influencers on OnlyFans

Trends in AI and Social Media

The intersection of artificial intelligence and social media is shaping the future of how content is created and consumed, particularly on platforms like OnlyFans. As creators look to leverage AI influencers, several key trends are emerging that can help maximize earnings and engage audiences more effectively. Understanding these trends is crucial for anyone looking to make money on OnlyFans by creating an AI influencer.

One of the most exciting trends is the rise of hyper-personalized content. AI algorithms can analyze user data to create tailored experiences that resonate with individual preferences. This means AI influencers can deliver content that feels personal and relevant, driving higher engagement rates. By utilizing tools that harness this technology, creators can ensure their AI influencers connect deeply with subscribers, resulting in increased loyalty and, ultimately, more revenue.

Another significant trend is the incorporation of augmented reality (AR) and virtual reality (VR) in social media interactions. As technologies advance, AI influencers can offer immersive experiences that go beyond traditional content. Imagine an AI influencer hosting a virtual meet-and-greet or an exclusive live show where fans can interact in real-time. This level of engagement not only captivates an audience but also opens up new monetization avenues, encouraging fans to pay for unique experiences that only an AI influencer can provide.

The influence of data analytics in shaping content strategies cannot be overstated. AI tools provide creators with insights into what content performs best, which demographics are most engaged, and how to optimize posting schedules. By analyzing these metrics, creators can refine their approach, ensuring they produce content that drives subscriptions and boosts earnings on OnlyFans. This data-driven mindset is essential for anyone looking to stand out in a competitive landscape.

Furthermore, the emergence of ethical AI is a trend that cannot be ignored. As audiences become more aware of the implications of AI in their lives, creators who prioritize transparency and ethical considerations in their AI influencer's identity will likely gain trust and build stronger relationships with their followers. By aligning AI creation with ethical standards, creators can foster a community that values authenticity, leading to sustained engagement and higher revenue in the long run.

In summary, the trends in AI and social media are not just exciting; they are transformative for anyone looking to make money on OnlyFans through AI influencers. From hyper-personalized content to immersive experiences and data-driven strategies, the opportunities are vast. As these trends continue to evolve, leveraging them effectively will be key to unlocking the full potential of AI influencers on the platform. Embrace these changes, and watch your OnlyFans journey soar to new heights!

Innovations on OnlyFans

In the rapidly evolving landscape of digital content creation, innovations on OnlyFans are transforming how creators engage with their audience and monetize their content. As more individuals venture into the world of AI influencers, the platform is becoming a hub for creativity and financial opportunity. From personalized interactions to immersive experiences, the advancements in technology are enabling creators to push the boundaries of what's possible, allowing them to stand out in a crowded marketplace.

One of the most exciting innovations on OnlyFans is the integration of artificial intelligence into content creation. AI influencers are not just avatars; they are dynamic characters that can interact with subscribers in real-time. With AI-driven chatbots, creators can maintain a constant presence, providing tailored responses that foster a deeper connection. This level of engagement not only keeps subscribers coming back but also increases the likelihood of upselling premium content. The ability to create a persona that feels real and relatable opens new avenues for storytelling and audience engagement.

Another game-changing innovation is the use of augmented reality (AR) and virtual reality (VR) content. Creators can now offer immersive experiences that allow subscribers to feel as if they are part of a unique world. Imagine a subscriber putting on VR goggles and stepping into a virtual concert or an exclusive behind-the-scenes tour of a photo shoot. These experiences elevate the content beyond traditional images and videos, creating memorable moments that subscribers are eager to share and discuss. This kind of innovation not only enhances user experience but also drives higher subscription rates and retention.

Moreover, data analytics tools are empowering creators to make informed decisions about their content strategy. By analyzing subscriber behavior and preferences, creators can tailor their offerings to meet the demands of their audience. Whether it's adjusting posting schedules, refining content themes, or exploring new niches, understanding what resonates with subscribers is crucial for maximizing revenue. This data-driven approach takes the guesswork out of content creation, allowing creators to focus on what they do best while ensuring their efforts translate into financial success.

Finally, collaborations between AI influencers and traditional creators are starting to gain traction, creating a perfect blend of innovation and authenticity. By partnering with established creators, AI influencers can tap into existing fan bases, while traditional creators can leverage the novelty of AI to attract new subscribers. These collaborations not only enrich the content available on OnlyFans but also pave the way for groundbreaking projects that capture the imagination of audiences worldwide. The fusion of human and AI creativity is set to redefine the landscape of content creation and monetization on platforms like OnlyFans, making it an exciting time to be part of this dynamic industry.

Preparing for the Future

Preparing for the future in the realm of OnlyFans and AI influencers is an exhilarating journey filled with opportunities. As you dive into creating an AI influencer, it's essential to stay ahead of the curve by understanding the rapidly evolving landscape of digital content creation. The marketplace is dynamic, and with the right strategies, you can position yourself as a frontrunner in this innovative space. Embrace the excitement of potential as you prepare to harness the power of AI technology, which is revolutionizing how content is produced and consumed.

First and foremost, investing time in understanding your target audience is crucial. Research their preferences, behaviors, and interests to tailor your AI influencer's persona effectively. By creating a character that resonates with your audience, you unlock the potential for higher engagement and loyalty. Utilize analytics tools to gather insights that will guide your content strategy. The more you know about your audience, the more effectively you can craft unique and captivating experiences that keep them coming back for more. This foundational step will set the stage for your success on OnlyFans.

Next, focus on the technological aspects of your AI influencer. Familiarize yourself with the latest advancements in AI and digital media to ensure your content stands out. Platforms and tools that facilitate the creation of lifelike avatars and engaging storylines are continually evolving. By keeping your skills sharp and exploring new software and applications, you can enhance your production quality and appeal. The goal is to create an AI influencer that feels real and relatable, blurring the lines between artificial intelligence and genuine human connection.

Networking within the community is another vital component of your preparation. Engage with other creators, industry experts, and influencers to share ideas, collaborate, and gain insights. Attend virtual events, join online forums, and participate in social media discussions to expand your reach and knowledge. Building relationships with fellow creators will not only inspire you but may also lead to potential partnerships that can amplify your success. In this interconnected world, collaboration can open doors to new audiences and innovative ideas.

Finally, always keep an eye on future trends and innovations in the space. The digital landscape is ever-changing, and the ability to adapt is essential for long-term success. Stay informed about emerging technologies, shifts in consumer behavior, and industry developments. By anticipating changes and being willing to pivot your strategy, you will remain relevant and competitive. Preparing for the future means being proactive rather than reactive, ensuring that your AI influencer remains at the forefront of the OnlyFans scene. Embrace this exhilarating journey, and watch as your vision transforms into a thriving reality.

Chapter 10: Conclusion and Next Steps

Recap of Key Takeaways

In this vibrant journey through the world of OnlyFans and AI influencers, we've uncovered some powerful strategies and insights that can elevate your earning potential. The key takeaway is the immense opportunity presented by AI technology to create captivating and engaging content that resonates with audiences. By leveraging AI, you can craft unique personas that cater to specific niches, drawing in subscribers who are eager for fresh and innovative experiences. This not only diversifies your content but also enhances your appeal in an increasingly crowded marketplace.

Another crucial point is the importance of understanding your target audience. Knowing what your potential subscribers crave allows you to tailor your AI influencer's content to meet their desires. Whether it's fitness tips, beauty tutorials, or exclusive behind-the-scenes glimpses into a luxurious lifestyle, the more aligned your content is with audience interests, the more likely you are to convert viewers into loyal subscribers. Engaging with your audience and incorporating their feedback into your content can create a community feel, fostering long-term relationships that benefit your bottom line.

Equally important is the role of consistency in your content strategy. Maintaining a regular posting schedule not only keeps your audience engaged but also establishes your AI influencer as a reliable source of entertainment or information. Utilizing AI tools to automate content creation and scheduling can provide you with the flexibility to focus on other aspects of your business. This strategic approach allows for a steady flow of content, ensuring you remain relevant and top-of-mind for your subscribers.

Don't forget the power of marketing and promotion. Promoting your AI influencer across various social media platforms can significantly expand your reach. Create eye-catching teasers and snippets that highlight the unique aspects of your content. Collaborating with other creators or influencers can also amplify your visibility and draw in new subscribers. Remember, the more eyes on your brand, the greater your potential for success on OnlyFans.

Finally, embracing innovation and staying ahead of trends is essential for long-term success. The landscape of social media and content creation is ever-evolving, and being adaptable will set you apart from the competition. Keep an eye on emerging technologies and trends within the AI space, as they can provide new tools and methods for enhancing your content. By continuously learning and evolving, you can ensure that your AI influencer remains a captivating presence on OnlyFans, driving both engagement and revenue.

Setting Goals for Your AI Influencer

Setting goals for your AI influencer is the first and perhaps the most crucial step in your journey to success on OnlyFans. Clear, specific, and achievable goals will serve as your roadmap, guiding you through the intricate landscape of content creation and audience engagement. Start by defining what you want to achieve with your AI influencer. Are you aiming for a certain number of subscribers, a specific income target, or perhaps a level of engagement with your audience? Knowing the answers to these questions will not only motivate you but will also help you measure your progress as you move forward.

Once you have a general idea of your goals, break them down into smaller, manageable milestones. For example, if your ultimate goal is to reach 10,000 subscribers, set intermediate targets like gaining your first 1,000 subscribers within the first month. This will make the journey feel less daunting and more achievable. Celebrate these small victories as they come; each milestone reached is a testament to your hard work and dedication. By keeping your goals segmented, you can maintain momentum and stay enthusiastic about your progress.

Next, consider the content strategy that will help you achieve your goals. Align your content with the interests of your target audience while ensuring it reflects the personality and brand of your AI influencer. Engaging content is the heart of any successful OnlyFans venture. Think about what types of posts will resonate most with your audience—whether it's risqué photos, behind-the-scenes videos, or interactive Q&A sessions. The more you tailor your content to meet your goals and audience preferences, the more likely you are to boost your subscriber count and income.

Don't forget to continually assess and adjust your goals as you gather data about your performance. The digital landscape is always evolving, and flexibility will be key to your success. Use analytics tools provided by OnlyFans to track your growth, engagement rates, and subscriber feedback. If you notice certain types of content performing better than others, adapt your strategy accordingly. Setting goals isn't a one-time task; it requires regular reviews and adjustments to ensure you stay on the path to success.

Finally, remember that persistence is essential. The journey to becoming a successful AI influencer on OnlyFans will have its ups and downs. There may be times when growth feels stagnant or when you encounter challenges that seem insurmountable. Stay focused on your goals and remind yourself of the passion that drove you to create your AI influencer in the first place. With enthusiasm, a clear vision, and a commitment to your goals, you'll not only navigate the obstacles but also thrive in the vibrant world of OnlyFans.

Resources for Further Learning

To truly excel in the realm of OnlyFans and maximize your earning potential with AI influencers, it's essential to continuously expand your knowledge and skill set. Fortunately, a wealth of resources is available to help you navigate this exciting landscape. From online courses to community forums, these resources can provide you with the tools and insights needed to create a successful AI influencer that captivates audiences and drives revenue.

Online platforms like Udemy and Coursera offer specialized courses focused on digital marketing, content creation, and artificial intelligence. These courses often feature industry experts who share their insights, tips, and tricks for success. By enrolling in these programs, you can gain a deeper understanding of how to leverage AI technology to create engaging content and optimize your strategies for audience engagement. Investing in your education can pay off significantly as you implement what you learn to boost your OnlyFans earnings.

In addition to formal courses, numerous blogs and podcasts focus on the intersection of AI and social media. These resources are invaluable for staying up-to-date with the latest trends, tools, and techniques in the industry. Engaging with content from thought leaders can inspire innovative ideas for your AI influencer. Following these experts on social media platforms can also foster a sense of community, allowing you to connect with others who share your passion for creating and monetizing AI-driven content.

Networking is another critical resource for further learning. Joining forums and communities dedicated to OnlyFans and AI influencers can provide you with invaluable insights and support from like-minded individuals. Participating in discussions, asking questions, and sharing your experiences can lead to new collaborations and partnerships that can elevate your brand. Engaging with others in your niche can help you discover new strategies and approaches that you might not have considered on your own.

Finally, don't underestimate the power of experimentation and analysis. As you create content with your AI influencer, take the time to analyze the performance of your posts and campaigns. Utilize analytics tools to track engagement metrics and audience behavior. This hands-on learning will provide you with practical insights that can inform your future decisions and strategies. Remember, the journey to mastering OnlyFans and AI influencers is ongoing, and each step you take opens doors to new possibilities. Embrace the resources available to you, and watch your success unfold!

www.ingramcontent.com/pod-product-compliance
Lightning Source LLC
Chambersburg PA
CBHW070138230526
45472CB00004B/1588